I0017729

# Google
# Pixel 8
# and 8 Pro

## User Guide

# Google Pixel 8 and 8 Pro

## User Guide

A Complete User Manual for Beginners to Use and Master the Google Pixel 8 Series, Including Trouble Shooting Hacks, Tips, and Tricks for the Latest Android

## DAVID WEST

Google Pixel 8 and 8 Pro User Guide

Copyright © 2023 by David West

All Rights Reserved.

No part of this book may be reproduced, stored in a retrievable system, transmitted in any form, or by any means, electronic, mechanical, photocopying, recording, or otherwise, without prior written permission from the author.

# CONTENTS

# CHAPTER 1

# Introduction to the Google Pixel 8 and 8 Pro

The newly remodeled Google Pixel 8 and 8 Pro phone is designed with an AI that helps to provide users with an even better personal experience. Google

Tensor G3 powers it and has a new **temperature sensor** feature to help you check a room's or object's temperature. It has the following unique features;

## Smart designs

The Google Pixel 8 and 8 Pro come in a better design than the previous email; it has a better-designed camera bar, beautiful metal finish, and contoured edges, and they're smaller than the Google Pixel 7 for a more fantastic feel on the palms, it is also 100% recyclable. The Google Pixel 8 and 8 Pros come with brighter and better displays than the previous design, making them easier to use in open sunlight and dark places; the Google Pixel 8 comes in three colors: Rose, Hazel, and obsidian, while the eight pros have a 6.7-inch supa acta display and come in porcelain, bay and obsidian color.

## AI improved

The new phone gets work done easier and faster with the aid of its AI feature; it allows users to use voice to type, edit, and send messages of any kind in any language; its call screening feature also helps to block and reduce spam calls.

**Seven years update**

The Google Pixel 8 and 8 Pro come with seven years of software updates on Android OS, security updates, and airdrop features.

**Improved camera**

It has a better camera update for taking quality photos and videos; it has features like best take, magic editor, a magic eraser that helps to remove unwanted noise in a video background, and many more; it also comes with bigger ultra lenses with a macro focus that helps you take best angles of photos.

# Basic Features of the Google Pixel 8 and 8 Pro

| Features | Google Pixel 8 | Google Pixel 8 Pro |
|---|---|---|
| RAM | 8GB RAM | 12GB RAM |
| STORAGE | 128GB, 256GB | 128GB, 256GB, 512GB, 1TB |
| BATTERY | 4575 MAH | 5050 MAH |
| OPERATING SYSTEM | ANDRIOD 14 | ANDROID 14 |
| DISPLAY | 6.2 INCH | 6.7 INCH |
| PRICE | $699 | $999 |

# CHAPTER 2

# Getting Started

## Unboxing the Google Pixel 8 and 8 Pro

The first step is to unbox the Pixel. Remove the phone from the packaging and remove all the accessories, including the charger, USB cable, and SIM card tool. Then, turn the phone over and locate the SIM card slot. Using the SIM card tool, open the SIM card tray and insert the SIM card. Make sure the gold contacts on the SIM card are facing down. Once the SIM card is inserted, close the tray.

# Turning on the Google Pixel 8 and 8 Pro

The next step is to turn on the Pixel. Press the Power button until the Google logo appears on the screen. After the logo appears, release the Power button. The Pixel will then begin the setup process. It's important to note that the initial setup may take some time, so be patient.

# Charging the Google Pixel 8 and 8 Pro

First, take the charging cable that came with your Pixel and plug it into a power outlet. Then, plug the other end of the cable into the charging port on your Pixel. You should see a charging indicator on the screen of your Pixel. Once the Pixel is fully charged, the indicator will disappear.

# Setting up the Google Pixel 8 and 8 Pro

Once the Pixel has started up, you'll see a "Welcome" screen. From here, you'll need to choose a language. To do this:

1. Tap the arrow next to the language you want to use.

2. Tap "Next." The Pixel will then ask you to connect to a WiFi network.

3. Tap the network you want to use and enter the password, if necessary.

4. Tap "Next" once you're connected.

## Setting up a Google Account

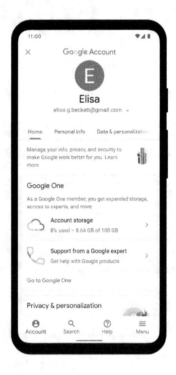

If you have a Google account, tap "Sign in" and enter your email address and password. If you don't have a Google account, tap "Create account" and follow the on-screen instructions to create one.

## Setting up Security

The next step is to set up security. This is important, as it will help protect your Pixel and keep your information safe. The Pixel will ask you to set up a PIN, password, or pattern lock. Please choose the option you prefer and follow the instructions on the screen to set it up. The Pixel will ask if you want to set up "Device Protection." This is an important feature that helps protect your data if your Pixel is lost or stolen. Tap "Next" to set it up.

## Transferring Data to Your New Pixel 8 and 8 Pro

First, make sure your old Pixel is turned on and unlocked. Then, connect the Quick Switch Adapter to your new Pixel. Next, connect the other end of the adapter to your old Pixel. Finally, follow the on-

screen instructions to transfer your data; the transfer process can take some time, so be patient. Once the transfer is complete, you can use your new Pixel with all your old Pixel data. Another method you can use in data transferring If you don't have the Quick Switch Adapter, you can use the "Android Switch" app. This app lets you transfer data wirelessly from your old Pixel to your new Pixel. You can download the app from the Google Play Store. To use these, first ensure your old Pixel is connected to a WiFi network. Then, open the Android Switch app on your old

Pixel. Tap "Transfer" and then "New device." Follow the on-screen instructions to connect your old Pixel to your new Pixel. Once the connection is established, select the data you want to transfer and tap "Start." The data will then be transferred to your new Pixel.

## Connecting the Google Pixel 8 or 8 Pro to WiFi

First, open the Settings app on your Pixel. Then, tap "Network & internet." Next, tap "WiFi." Then, make sure the WiFi switch is turned on. Your Pixel will then scan for available WiFi networks. Tap the name of the WiFi network you want to connect to. Finally, enter the password for the network and tap "Connect."

# Connecting the Google Pixel to Bluetooth

To connect your Pixel to Bluetooth, first open the Settings app. Then, tap "Connected devices" and then "Bluetooth." Make sure the Bluetooth switch is turned on. Your Pixel will then scan for available Bluetooth devices. Tap the device name you want to connect to and follow the on-screen instructions to complete the connection.

## Using the Headphone Jack of the Google Pixel

To use the headphone jack on your Pixel, first locate the headphone jack on the bottom of the device. Then, take your headphones and plug the audio cable into the headphone jack. Ensure the headphones are turned on, then adjust the volume to your desired level.

## Mobile Network Settings on the Google Pixel

The Google Pixel supports dual SIM cards, which means you can use two different SIM cards. You can use the SIM card manager to switch between the two SIM cards and to manage their settings.

To access the mobile network settings on your Pixel, open the Settings app. Then, tap "Network & Internet" and "Mobile network." You'll see a list of options for your mobile network, such as your carrier, network mode, and data usage.

## Carrier settings

In this setting, you can select your carrier from a list of available carriers. Next is network mode. This setting allows you to select the type of network you want to use, such as LTE, 3G, or 2G. The data usage setting lets you track how much data you've used, and the cellular data setting allows you to turn cellular data on or off.

## Selecting network type

The following setting is "Preferred network type." This setting lets you choose between 4G and 3G networks. "Roaming" allows you to turn on or off roaming while traveling. "WiFi calling" enables you to make calls over a WiFi connection instead of a cellular network. The "Call settings" option allows you to manage your call settings, such as call waiting, caller ID, and more.

## Advanced settings

The "Advanced" setting lets you manage a few more advanced options, such as the Access Point Name (APN) and the IP address. The APN is a setting that allows your device to connect to your carrier's network. The IP address is a unique identifier for your device on a network.

## Adaptive Connectivity

Adaptive Connectivity is a feature available on the Google Pixel device. It's designed to improve the quality of your connection by automatically switching between different networks, like 5G, 4G, and WiFi. This can be useful if you're in an area with poor network coverage by connecting to a more efficient network. Go to "Settings > Network and Internet > Adaptive Connectivity" to enable Adaptive Connectivity.

## How to Browse the Web on the Google Pixel

You can use Chrome's built-in browser to browse the web on your Pixel. Thump the Chrome icon on your home screen or the browser icon in the app drawer to open Chrome. To navigate a website, type the URL into the address bar at the top of the screen and tap "Go."

## Battery and Power Management on Google Pixel

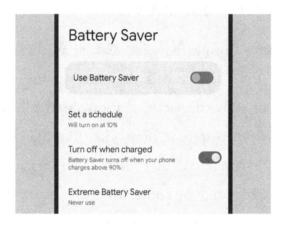

The Pixel has several features to help you manage your battery life. The "Battery Saver" mode can be enabled to extend your battery life. You can also monitor your battery usage and see which apps use the most power. The "Adaptive Battery" feature also learns your usage patterns over time and optimizes your battery accordingly. The "Battery Health" feature monitors the health of your Pixel's battery over time. This feature can help you determine when to replace your battery. The Pixel also has a "Fast charging" feature that lets you quickly charge your device. To activate battery and power management features

> To enable "Battery Saver," open the Settings app and tap "Battery." Then, tap the "Battery Saver" switch to turn it on. You can also choose when Battery Saver should automatically turn on. To enable "Adaptive Battery," open the Settings app and tap "Battery." Then, tap the "Adaptive Battery" switch to turn it on.

> To check the battery health of your Google Pixel, first open the Settings app. Then, tap "Battery." On this screen, you'll see information about your Pixel's battery, including the current battery level, usage since the last charge, and estimated battery life remaining. You'll also see a breakdown of how your battery is used, including how much each app uses.

> The adaptive charging feature on your Google Pixel learns from your charging habits and optimizes the charging process to extend the battery's lifespan. To turn on adaptive charging, first open the Settings app. Then, tap "Battery" and scroll down to "Adaptive charging." Here,

you can toggle adaptive charging on or off. You can also set a regular alarm in the Clock app to wake up to, and adaptive charging will learn when you typically unplug your Pixel in the morning.

## Storage and Memory Management

The "Storage" feature allows you to see how much storage space is available and how it's being used. You can also view and manage your files in the "Files" app. Additionally, the "Memory" feature allows you to see how much RAM is used and which apps use the most memory. You can also "Free up space" by clearing the cache and storage for specific apps.

► To enable "Storage" features, open the Settings app and tap "Storage." Then, you can manage your storage usage from the main Storage screen. To enable "Memory" features, open the Settings app and tap "Memory." Then, you can view and manage your apps' memory usage.

# How to Make and Receive Calls with the Google Pixel 8 and 8 Pro

First, open the Phone app and tap the "Phone" icon. Then, you can enter a number and tap the "Call" button to make a call. To receive a call, you'll need to open the Phone app and wait for the incoming call notification to appear. Then, you can answer the call by tapping the "Answer" button.

## Managing contacts

Managing your contacts on the Google Pixel is straightforward. First, open the Contacts app. Then, tap "Contacts" to view your list of contacts. From here, you can tap a contact to view their details, add a new contact, or delete a contact. You can also tap "Favorites" to view your favorite contacts or "Groups" to organize your contacts into groups.

## Blocking spam calls

First, open the Phone app and tap "More" in the bottom right corner. Then, tap "Settings" and scroll down to "Caller ID & spam." Here, you can enable "Filter suspected spam calls" to block spam calls. You can also block specific numbers by tapping "Block numbers" and adding the number you want to block.

## Call forwarding

To configure call forwarding on your Google Pixel, open the Phone app and tap "Settings." Then, tap "Call settings." Next, tap "Call forwarding." Here, you can choose which types of calls to forward and enter the phone number to which you want to forward calls. You can forward all calls when your phone is busy, calls when you don't answer, or when your phone is turned off.

## Call screening

Call screening is a feature that helps you avoid unwanted calls by screening callers before you answer. To enable call screening, open the Phone app and tap "Settings." Then, select "Spam and Call Screen." You can toggle on "Call Screen" and customize the settings for call screening on this screen.

## Enabling hold for me mode

Hold for me mode is a feature that can help you avoid long wait times when calling customer service or other busy lines. To enable hold for me mode, open the Phone app and tap "Settings." Then, select "Hold for me." You can toggle on "Hold for me" to enable the feature on this screen. When you're on a call, and the other line puts you on hold, you'll see an option to activate hold for me mode.

## Enabling call notifications on other devices

Call notification on other devices is a feature that allows you to receive call notifications on your other devices, such as a tablet or smartwatch. To enable this feature, open the Settings app and select "Phone." Then, select "Call notifications on other devices." You can toggle "Call notifications on other devices" on this screen and choose which devices you want to receive call notifications.

## Call history

Call history is a feature that allows you to view your recent calls and the call details for each call. To view your call history, open the Phone app and tap "Recents." You can see all of your recent calls on this screen, including missed, answered, and outgoing calls. You can also tap on a call to see the details, such as the phone number and call duration.

## How to Send and Receive Messages with the Google Pixel 8 and 8 Pro

First, open the Messages app and tap the "Compose" button to create a new message. Then, enter the recipient's number or name and type your message. To send the message, tap the "Send" button. To receive a message, you'll need to open the Messages app and wait for the incoming message notification to appear. Then, you can tap the notification to view the message.

## How to Listen to and Access Music and Podcast

First, open the Music app and tap the "Music" tab. Then, you can browse your music library and select the song or album you want to listen to. To play a song or album, tap the play button. To listen to a podcast, open the Podcasts app and browse or search for the podcast you want to listen to. Then, tap the play button to start playing the podcast.

► To create a podcast playlist, open the Podcasts app and tap the "Podcasts" tab. Then, tap the "New" button in the upper right corner of the screen. This will open the New Playlist screen. You can name your playlist in the New Playlist screen and tap "Create." Then, you can add podcasts to your playlist by tapping the "Add" button next to each podcast. You can also reorder your podcasts in the playlist by tapping and dragging them into the desired position. To listen to your playlist, Tap the "play" button.

# CHAPTER 3

# Customizing the Google Pixel 8 and 8 Pro Device

## Personalizing the Home Screen of the Google Pixel 8

First, tap and hold a space on your home screen. Then, select "Wallpaper & style" from the menu that appears. On the Wallpaper & style screen, you can select a wallpaper and customize the theme and style of your home screen. You can also add widgets to your home screen by tapping and holding a space on the home screen and selecting "Widgets" from the menu.

## Adding a Widget to the Google Pixel

Widgets are a great way to personalize your home screen and quickly access your favorite apps and information. To add a widget, follow these steps:

- ► Tap and hold a space on your home screen.
- ► Select "Widgets" from the menu that appears.
- ► Browse the available widgets and select the one you want to add.
- ► Move slowly and drop the widget onto your home screen.
- ► Resize and reposition the widget to your liking.

You can add as many widgets as you like to your home screen.

# Changing the wallpaper of the Google Pixel

First, tap and hold a space on your home screen. Then, select "Wallpaper & style" from the menu. On the Wallpaper & style screen, tap "Wallpaper" and select the type of wallpaper you want. You can choose from the default wallpapers or your photos. You can also choose from different wallpaper categories, like landscapes or abstracts. Once you've selected the wallpaper you want, tap "Set wallpaper" to apply it.

# Customizing the Lock Screen of the Google Pixel

You can customize your Pixel's lock screen! To start, open the Settings app and select "Lock screen." From there, you can customize the following:

- **Wallpaper:** Choose a wallpaper for your lock screen.

- **Clock:** Choose the style and size of the clock on your lock screen.

- **Lock screen message:** Add a personal message or information to your lock screen.

- **Wake screen:** Choose how your Pixel wakes up when you touch the screen.

- **Always On Display:** Customize the Always On Display on your Pixel.

## Choosing the Background Image for the Lock Screen

First, tap "Wallpaper" on the Lock screen settings screen. Then, you can choose from the default lock screen wallpapers or select "Gallery" to choose an image from your phone's gallery. You can also select "Photo Frame" to choose a dynamic wallpaper that changes based on the time of day or location. If you select "Photo Frame," you can customize the frequency and location settings.

## Customizing the Always On Display

First, open the Settings app and select "Display." Then, tap "Always On Display." From here, you can customize the following:

► Clock style
► Date style
► Font size
► Background image
► AOD theme
► AOD clock style
► AOD ambient brightness
► AOD screen duration
► AOD touch and hold
► AOD touch and hold duration

You can turn the Always on or Off Display feature from this menu.

► **Customizing the date style:** Tap "Date style" on the Always On Display settings screen. You can choose to display the date in digital or analog format. You can also choose to display the day of the week.

▶ **Customize the font size:** Tap "Font size" on the Always On Display settings screen. You can then choose from various font sizes, from small to large.

▶ **Customize the background image:** Tap "Background image" on the Always On Display settings screen. From here, you can choose from a variety of preset backgrounds, or you can choose your image from your photo library.

▶ **Customize the AOD theme:** Tap "AOD theme" on the Always On Display settings screen. You can choose from various themes, including light, dark, and dynamic.

▶ **Customize the AOD clock style:** Tap "AOD clock style" on the Always On Display settings screen. You can choose from analog, digital, and monogram clock styles.

▶ **Customize the AOD ambient brightness:** Tap "AOD ambient brightness" on the Always On Display settings screen. You can choose from three ambient brightness levels: low, medium, and high.

▶ **Customize the AOD touch and hold feature:** Tap "AOD touch and hold" on the Always On Display settings screen. You can choose how long the AOD stays on when you touch and hold the screen.

▶ **Customize the AOD screen duration:** Tap "AOD screen duration" on the Always On Display settings screen. From here, you can choose how long the AOD stays on after you wake up your device.

▶ **Accessibility:** Tap "Accessibility" on the Always On Display settings screen. From here, you can customize various accessibility settings, including text-to-speech, font size, and color inversion.

▶ **Accessibility Menu:** Tap "Accessibility Menu" on the Always On Display settings screen. You can customize the accessibility menu to make it easier to use your device.

▶ **App Permissions:** Tap "App Permissions" on the Always On Display settings screen. From here, you can choose which apps have permission to access the Always On Display.

## Customizing Gestures

Tap "Gestures" on the Display settings screen. Then, tap "Home." You can choose whether to use the Home gesture by swiping up from the bottom of the screen or the bottom center of the screen.

## Customizing the Buttons

Tap "Buttons" on the Display settings screen. Here, you can customize the behavior of the power button, the volume button, and the virtual navigation bar.

► **Customizing the power button:** Tap "Power button" on the Buttons settings screen. You can choose whether to power off your device, open the Assistant, or take a screenshot when you press and hold the Power button.

▶ **Customizing the volume buttons:** Tap "Volume buttons" on the Buttons settings screen. Here, you can choose what happens when you press the volume buttons. You can choose to control media volume, call volume, ringtone volume, alarm volume, or all volumes.

▶ **Customizing the virtual navigation buttons:** Tap "Virtual navigation buttons" on the Buttons settings screen. You can choose between the traditional three-button layout or the navigation gestures layout. With the three-button layout, you can customize the functions of the Back, Home, and Recents buttons. With the navigation gestures layout, you can customize the gestures that perform the same functions.

# Customizing the Sounds and Vibration

Tap "Sounds and vibration" on the Display settings screen. You can customize various sounds and vibrations here, including ringtone, notification sound, and touch sound.

## Customizing ringtone

Tap "Ringtone" on the Sounds and Vibration settings screen to choose a ringtone. You can choose from various pre-loaded ringtones or tap "Add ringtone" to choose a song from your music library.

## Customizing notification sounds

Tap "Notification sound" on the Sounds and Vibration settings screen. You can choose from pre-loaded notification sounds like the ringtone or add your own.

## Managing notifications on the lock screen

To manage notifications on the lock screen of your Google Pixel, first open the Settings app and tap

"Notifications." Then, tap "Lock screen notifications." Here, you can hide or show sensitive content, which apps can show notifications on the lock screen, and whether to show or hide notification icons. You can also choose whether to show or hide notification previews, and you can toggle on "Do not disturb" to silence notifications.

## Customizing touch sounds

Tap "Touch sound" on the Sounds and Vibration settings screen. You can turn the touch sound on or off or choose a sound from a list of pre-loaded options.

## Customizing vibration sounds

Tap "Vibration" on the Sounds and Vibration settings screen. You can choose a vibration pattern for calls, notifications, and touch interaction.

## Adaptive Sound

Adaptive Sound is a feature that's available on the Google Pixel. It's designed to automatically adjust your phone's volume and sound quality based on your environment. This can be useful if you're in a noisy environment or want to save battery life by lowering the volume in a quiet place. Go to "Settings > Sound > Adaptive Sound" to enable Adaptive Sound.

## Customizing Display Settings

Tap "Display" on the Display settings screen. You can customize the display's size, resolution, font size, display zoom, color scheme, and more.

## Customizing font size

Tap "Font size" on the Display settings screen. Use the slider to adjust the font size to your liking. Next, let's customize the display zoom. Tap "Display zoom" on the Display settings screen. You can choose between Standard, Zoomed, and Max Zoom.

## Customizing the color scheme

Tap "Colors" on the Display settings screen. You can choose between Natural, Boosted, and Adaptive. Natural uses a color profile that closely matches the colors you see in real life. Boosted and Adaptive use a more vibrant color profile.

## Customizing the screen time out

Tap "Screen timeout" on the Display settings screen. Use the slider to select when you want your Pixel's screen to stay on after you stop interacting with it.

## Customizing brightness

Tap "Brightness" on the Display settings screen. Here, you can choose the brightness level of your

Pixel's screen. You can also choose to set adaptive brightness, which automatically adjusts the brightness of your screen based on the lighting conditions.

## Customizing night light

To turn on the night light feature on your Google Pixel, first open the Settings app. Then, tap "Display." Next, tap "Night light" and toggle it on. You can also adjust the schedule for when the night light turns on and off. You can also choose the color temperature for the night light, with the default being a warm color. The warmer the color, the less blue light the screen emits.

## Customizing adaptive brightness

Tap "Adaptive brightness" on the Display settings screen. This setting automatically adjusts the brightness of your Pixel's display based on the lighting conditions around you.

## Customizing dark theme

Tap "Dark theme" on the Display settings screen. You can always use the dark theme for your Pixel's display, from sunset to sunrise, or never.

## Customizing ambient display

Tap "Ambient display" on the Display settings screen. Ambient display shows limited information on your Pixel's screen when it's turned off.

## Customizing screen saver

Tap "Screen saver" on the Display settings screen. A screen saver is a static or animated image displayed when your Pixel is idle for a set period. You can choose from various screen savers or create your own.

## Customizing screen resolution

Tap "Screen resolution" on the Display settings screen. Screen resolution controls the sharpness and clarity of your Pixel's display. There are multiple resolution options to choose from.

## Customizing fonts style

Tap "Font style" on the Display settings screen. Font style controls the look of the text on your Pixel's display. You can choose from various font styles, including Sans Serif, Serif, and Monospace.

# Customizing Accounts and Syncing Data

To customize the account and syncing data, open the Settings app and tap "Accounts & sync." This screen displays a list of accounts that are synced with your Pixel. Tap an account to see its sync settings. You can choose which data types are synced with the account.

## Backing up and Restoring Data

The Google Pixel does have its backup service, called Google One. You can enable Google One by opening the Settings app and tapping "System." Then, tap "Backup" and toggle "Back up to Google Drive." This will back up your data to Google Drive. To restore your data from a backup, open the Settings app and tap "System." Then, tap "Advanced" and "Reset options." Finally, tap "Erase all data (factory reset)" and follow the on-screen instructions.

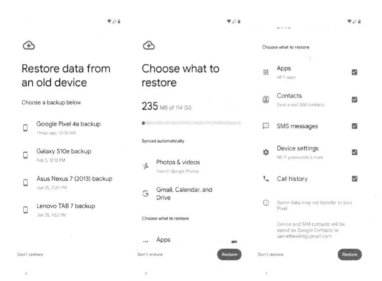

## Managing Location Setting

Managing the location setting on your Google Pixel is simple. First, open the Settings app and tap "Location." Here, you can choose whether to turn location services on or off. If location services are enabled, you can also choose the apps that have access to your location and choose the accuracy of your location. You can choose between battery saving, balanced, or high accuracy.

## Changing Language Setting

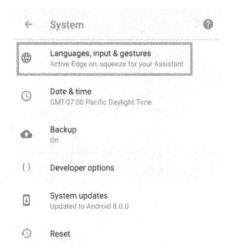

To change the language setting on your Google Pixel, first open the Settings app. Then, tap "System"

and "Languages & input." Here, you can choose the language you want your Pixel to be in. To add a new language, tap "Add a language" and choose the language you want to add. You can also set a default language and a preferred input method for each language.

## Changing Your Time Zone

To change your Google Pixel's time zone, open the Settings app and tap "System." Then, tap "Date & time." Here, you can toggle "Automatic date & time" to automatically set your Pixel's time zone based on location. You can also manually change the time zone by tapping "Time zone" and selecting the time zone you want.

# CHAPTER 4

# Apps

## How to Download Apps on the Google Pixel

It's easy to download apps on the Google Pixel. Go to the Google Play Store app and sign in with your Google account. Once you're signed in, tap the "Search" icon and search for the app you want to download. When you find the app, tap the "Install" button. The app will be downloaded and installed on your device.

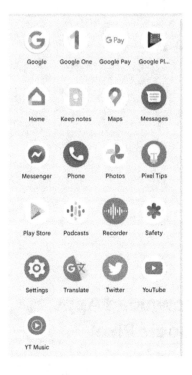

## How to Install the App on the Google Pixel

After you've found the app you want to install in the Google Play Store, here's how to install it. First, ensure you're connected to the internet, as you need an internet connection to download apps. Then, tap the "Install" button on the app's page. You'll be prompted to allow the app to access specific permissions, so you'll need to read through and accept the permissions before the app can be installed. The app will then start downloading, and once it's finished, you can open it and start using it.

## Creating Folders for Apps

Creating folders to organize your apps on your Google Pixel is simple. First, go to your home screen and touch and hold the app you want to move. After you've held the app for a few seconds, you'll see it start to "wiggle." This means it's ready to be moved. Then, drag the app over to the app you want to put it in a folder with. When you see a folder appear, release the app. This will create a new folder with the two apps you've selected.

## How to Open Apps

To open an app on your Google Pixel, you can use the home screen or the app drawer. On the home screen, tap the app you want to open. Alternatively, you can swipe up from the bottom of the home screen to open the app drawer. Then, find the app you want to open and tap on it. You can also use the search bar in the app drawer to find an app by name.

## How to Close Apps

You can use the app drawer to close an app on your Google Pixel. First, swipe up from the bottom of the home screen to open the app drawer. Then, find the app you want to close and swipe up on it. This will close the app. You can also close multiple apps simultaneously by swiping up multiple apps. You can also close apps by swiping them away in the recent apps view.

## Managing Apps

To manage your apps, open the Settings app and tap "Apps & notifications." This will show you a list of all the apps installed on your device. From here, you can tap on an app to see its details, clear its cache and data, or force it to stop. You can also tap "Uninstall" to remove an app from your device.

# Popular Apps on the Google Pixel 8 and 8 Pro

The Google Pixel comes with various apps pre-installed on the device. Some of the most popular apps include Google Chrome, Gmail, Google Drive, Google Maps, YouTube, Google Photos, and the Google Play Store.

## Google Chrome

To get started, open the Google Chrome app from the home screen. You'll be taken to the Chrome home page, which displays your most visited sites and recent tabs. To visit a website, enter the website address in the URL bar and press enter. The website will then load in the Chrome browser.

## Gmail

To start using Gmail on your Pixel, open the app from the home screen. You'll be taken to the Gmail inbox to see your recent emails. To view an email, tap on it. You can then read the email, reply, or perform other actions.

## Google Drive

To start with Google Drive, open the Google Drive app from the home screen. Once you're in the app, you'll see your files and folders organized into different categories, such as "My Drive," "Shared with me," and "Recent." To open a file, tap on it. You can then view, edit, or download the file.

## Google Maps

First, open the Google Maps app from the home screen. Once you're in the app, you'll see a map of your current location. You can zoom in and out by pinching and unpinching the screen. You can also search for a specific location by tapping the search bar and typing in the address or name of the place you want to find. Once you've found the location, you can get directions, view reviews, and more.

## YouTube

To start with YouTube, open the YouTube app from the home screen. The primary YouTube screen will show various recommended videos for you to watch. You can also search for specific videos by tapping the search bar and typing in a keyword or phrase. Once you find a video you want to watch, tap on it to begin playing. You can also use YouTube to subscribe to channels, create playlists, and more.

## Google Photos App

The first step is to open the Google Photos app from the home screen. When you open the app, you'll see your photos and videos organized into different categories, such as "Recents," "Albums," and "Archive." To view a photo or video, tap on it. You can then like, share, or edit the photo or video. Tap the "Create" button to create an album and select "Album."

## Google Play Store

First, open the Google Play Store app from the home screen. You'll see a variety of categories, such as "Apps," "Games," and "Movies & TV." Tap the appropriate category and browse the options to find an app, game, or movie. Once you've found something interesting, tap on it to learn more about it. You can install an app, game, or movie by tapping the "Install" button.

In addition to the apps that come pre-installed on the Pixel, there are many other apps that you can install from the Google Play Store. Some popular apps include WhatsApp, Instagram, Snapchat, Netflix, Spotify, and more.

## WhatsApp

WhatsApp is a popular messaging app that you can use to send messages, photos, videos, and more. To start, open the WhatsApp app and create an account by entering your phone number. You'll then be prompted to verify your number. Once you've verified your number, you can chat with your contacts.

## Instagram

Instagram is a social media app that allows you to share photos and videos with your followers. To get started, download the Instagram app and create an account. Once you've created your account, you can follow other users and post your photos and videos. To take a photo or video, tap the "+" icon in the bottom center of the screen.

## Snapchat

To get started with Snapchat, download the app and create an account. Once you've created your account, you can start taking photos and videos, called "snaps." To take a snap, tap the circular button at the bottom of the screen. You can add filters, text, or other effects to your snap. If you want to send your snap to a specific friend, tap the "Send To" button and choose the friend to whom you want to send it.

## Netflix

First, download the Netflix app and create an account. Once you have an account, you can start watching shows and movies. Tap the "Search" button and browse the different categories to find something to watch. When you find something you want to watch, tap on it and select "Play." You can then pause, rewind, and fast forward using the controls at the bottom of the screen.

## Spotify

You must download the Spotify app and create an account to use Spotify. Once you have an account, you can listen to music and podcasts. To find something to listen to, tap the "Search" button and browse the different categories. When you find something you want to listen to, tap on it and hit the "Play" button. You can also create playlists and follow other users on Spotify.

# CHAPTER 5

# Google Assistant

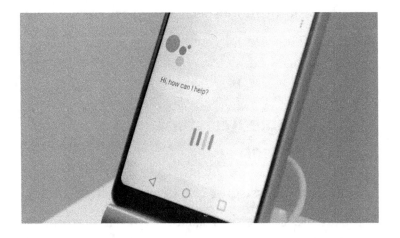

The Google Assistant is a virtual assistant built into your Google Pixel. You can use Google Assistant to set reminders, search the web, get directions, and more. To access the Google Assistant, press and hold the home button on your Pixel or say "Hey Google."

You can then speak your command or question to the Google Assistant.

## Using Google Assistant for the Weather

You can ask the Google Assistant for the current weather by saying, "Hey Google, what's the weather?" The Assistant will then provide you with the weather conditions and the forecast for the next few days. You can also ask for more specific weather information, such as "Hey Google, what's the chance of rain tomorrow?"

## Using Google Assistant for Translation

The Google Assistant can be an excellent tool for translation. To use the Assistant for translation, say, "Hey Google, how do you say ____ in ____?" For example, you could say, "Hey Google, how do you say 'hello' in French?" The Google Assistant will then provide you with the translation. You can also ask for more complex translations, such as complete sentences or phrases.

## Using Google Assistant for Calculation

You can use the Google Assistant to perform calculations by saying, "Hey Google, what is ____ plus ____?" or "Hey Google, what is ____ times ____?" The Assistant will then provide you with the answer. You can also ask the Assistant to do other calculations, such as division, multiplication, subtraction, and more.

## Using Google Assistant for Currency Conversion

The Google Assistant can help you convert currencies by saying, "Hey Google, how much is ____ in ____?" For example, you could say, "Hey Google, how much is 50 US dollars in euros?" The Assistant will then provide you with the conversion. You can also ask the Assistant to convert multiple currencies simultaneously, such as "Hey Google, how much is 100 US dollars, 50 euros, and 30 British pounds?"

## Using Google Assistant for Unit Conversion

The Google Assistant can help you convert between different units of measurement, such as ounces to grams, feet to meters, or miles to kilometers. To use the Assistant for unit conversion, say, "Hey Google, how many _____ is in _____?" For example, you could say, "Hey Google, how many ounces are in a pound?" or "Hey Google, how many miles are in a kilometer?" The Assistant will then provide you with the conversion.

## Using Google Assistant for Making Calls

To make a call, say, "Hey Google, call _____." The Assistant will then place a call to the number you requested. You can also ask the Assistant to call someone from your contacts by saying, "Hey, Google, call _____ from my contacts."

## Using Google Assistant for Navigation

The Google Assistant can help you navigate with Google Maps! To get started, say, "Hey, Google, navigate to ____." For example, you could say, "Hey Google, navigate to the nearest coffee shop." The Assistant will then provide you with turn-by-turn directions using Google Maps. You can also ask the Assistant for more specific directions, such as "Hey Google, navigate to the nearest coffee shop open 24 hours."

## Accessing Google Assistant Settings

To access the settings for the Google Assistant, open the Google app and tap the "More" tab. Then, tap "Settings" and select "Google Assistant." You can adjust the Assistant's voice, language, and other settings here.

## CHAPTER 6

# Security
# and Privacy

## Enabling SOS

Emergency SOS is a feature that allows you to call for help in an emergency quickly. To enable this feature, open the Settings app and select "Safety & emergency." Then, select "Emergency SOS." On this screen, you can toggle on "Emergency SOS" and choose whether to share your location when you call 911 automatically.

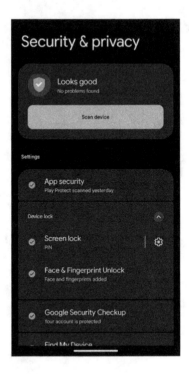

## Enabling Google Emergency Location Services

Google Emergency Location Services is a feature that allows your phone to automatically share your location with first responders if you call 911. To enable this feature, open the Settings app and select "Location." Then, select "Advanced." On this screen, you can toggle on "Emergency Location Service."

## Location Sharing

Location sharing is a feature that allows you to share your location with friends and family. To enable this feature, open the Google Maps app and tap "Location sharing" in the menu. On the location sharing screen, you can choose who you want to share your location with and for how long.

## Adding a PIN

Adding a PIN is a great way to add an extra layer of security to your device. To add a PIN, open the Settings app and select "Security." Then, select "Screen lock." You can add a PIN, pattern, password, or fingerprint as your screen lock on this screen.

## Adding a Password

Adding a password is another way to add an extra layer of security to your device. To add a password, open the Settings app and select "Security." Then, select "Screen lock." On this screen, choose "Password" and follow the instructions to set a password.

## Adding a Pattern

Adding a pattern is another way to secure your device. To add a pattern, open the Settings app and select "Security." Then, select "Screen lock." On this screen, choose "Pattern" and follow the instructions to set a pattern. A pattern is a sequence of dots you draw on the screen to unlock your device.

## Adding a Fingerprint

A fingerprint is another way to add an extra layer of security to your device. To add a fingerprint, open the Settings app and select "Security." Then, select "Screen lock." Choose "Fingerprint" on this screen and follow the instructions to set up your fingerprint. Your fingerprint will be used to unlock your device.

## Adding Face Recognition

Adding face recognition is another way to add an extra layer of security to your device. To add face recognition, open the Settings app and select "Security." Then, select "Screen lock." Choose "Face" on this screen and follow the instructions to set up face recognition. Your face will be used to unlock your device.

## Adding Face Unlock

Adding face unlock is similar to adding face recognition. The main difference is that face unlock is supported by the Android operating system, while face recognition is supported by the Pixel phone's hardware and software. Both methods can be used to secure your device.

## Smart Lock

A smart lock is a feature that allows you to keep your device unlocked when it's in a trusted place, such as your home or office. To turn on the smart lock, open the Settings app and select "Security." Then, select "Smart lock." On this screen, you can choose to enable smart locks based on your location, trusted devices, or trusted faces.

## Accessing Privacy Settings

Privacy settings allow you to control how much information is shared with Google and other apps. To access privacy settings, open the Settings app and select "Privacy." You can choose the apps that can access your location, camera, microphone, contacts, and other features on this screen. You can also review the privacy policies of your installed apps.

# CHAPTER 7

# Google Family Link App

The Google Pixel can be an excellent device for family communication and collaboration. You can create a family group in the Google Family Link app, which allows you to share photos, calendar events, reminders, and more with your family members. You can also set up screen time limits and content restrictions for children in the family group. The first step is downloading the Google Family Link app on your Pixel. Once you've done that, open the app and tap the "Add family member" button. You'll need to enter the child's name and date of birth. Once you've added the child to the family group, you can customize the settings for their account. You can set content restrictions, set screen time limits, and more. If you need to remove a member from the family group, Open the Family Link app and tap the menu button in the top left corner. Tap the "Manage family members" option and select the family member you want to remove. Tap the "Remove" button and confirm the removal. The family member will no longer have access to the family group features.

## Digital Wellbeing

Digital Wellbeing is a feature in the Family Link app that allows you to manage your child's digital habits. With Digital Wellbeing, you can set daily device usage limits, set timers for apps, block apps at bedtime, and more. This feature is designed to help your child find a healthy balance between their digital life and the rest of their life.

## Parental Controls

The Family Link app has several parental controls that you can use to manage your child's device usage. With these controls, you can:

- ► Block the installation of specific apps
- ► Filter content for YouTube and Google Search
- ► Disable location sharing for certain apps
- ► View a history of app usage
- ► Manage in-app purchases
- ► Manage screen time limits and device bedtime
- ► Receive notifications when your child unlocks their device or leaves a designated location.

If you have any questions about parental controls, you can find more information in the Family Link help center.

## Sharing Location with Family Members

The Family Link app allows you to share your child's location with other family members. This is a great way to keep track of your child's whereabouts and ensure they're safe. To share your child's location, open the Family Link app and go to the "Settings" tab. Then, select the "Location" option and enable the "Share child's location" option.

# CHAPTER 8

# Accessibility Setting

In addition to the accessibility settings for the Google Assistant, the Google Pixel phone also has various accessibility features. To access these settings, go to the Settings app and select "Accessibility." From there, you can turn on features like TalkBack, which provides audible feedback for everything you touch, or Live Transcribe, which converts speech to text in real-time. There are also various other features to make your phone more straightforward.

## Enabling TalkBack

To enable TalkBack, open the Settings app and select "Accessibility." Then, tap "TalkBack" and toggle it on. Once TalkBack is enabled, your phone will provide audible feedback for everything you touch. TalkBack will also read the text on your screen out loud.

## Enabling Caption

To enable captions, open the Settings app and select "Accessibility." Then, select "Captions." You can toggle "Captions" on this screen to enable captions for all media played on your phone. You can customize the captions by adjusting the size, color, and opacity.

## Enabling Color Correction

Enabling color correction is easy! First, open the Settings app and select "Accessibility." Then, select "Color correction." You can toggle on "Color correction" to enable the feature. You can also adjust the intensity and tint of the color correction.

## Enabling Text Magnification

To enable text magnification, open the Settings app and select "Accessibility." Then, select "Text magnification." You can toggle on "Text magnification" to enable the feature here. Once enabled, you can tap and hold on to any text to enlarge it. You can also use two fingers to zoom in and out of the text.

## Enabling High Contrast

To enable high contrast mode, open the Settings app and select "Accessibility." Then, select "High contrast." You can toggle on "High contrast mode" to enable the feature on this screen. This will make text and other elements on your screen more visible by increasing the contrast between colors.

## Enabling Color Inversion

Color inversion is another accessibility feature that can make your screen easier to see. To enable color inversion, open the Settings app and select "Accessibility." Then, select "Color inversion." You can toggle on "Color inversion" to enable the feature on this screen. This will invert the colors on your screen, making it easier to see certain elements.

## Enabling Show Button Shapes

Showing button shapes is a great accessibility feature for users who have difficulty seeing the edges of buttons. To enable this feature, open the Settings app and select "Accessibility." Then, select "Button shapes." On this screen, you can toggle on "Show button shapes" to enable the feature. This will add a border around buttons to make them easier to see and interact with.

## Enabling Reduce Motion

Reduce motion is an accessibility feature that reduces the amount of animation and movement on your screen. To enable this feature, open the Settings app and select "Accessibility." Then, select "Reduce motion." You can toggle on "Reduce motion" to enable the feature on this screen. This will make your screen easier to look at by reducing the amount of animation.

## Enabling Reduce Animations

Reduce animations is a related accessibility feature that reduces the amount of animations on your screen. To enable this feature, open the Settings app and select "Accessibility." Then, select "Reduce animations." You can toggle on "Reduce anima-tions" to enable the feature on this screen. This will make your screen easier to look at by reducing the number of animations that appear.

## Enabling Bedtime Mode

Bedtime mode is an accessibility feature that helps you get a good night's sleep by reducing distractions and light on your phone. To enable bedtime mode, open the Settings app and select "Digital wellbeing & parental controls." Then, select "Bedtime mode" and toggle it on. You can then customize the hours during which bedtime mode is enabled and select whether you want your screen to turn grayscale and whether you want to silence notifications.

## Enabling Wind Down

Wind down is another digital wellbeing feature that helps you get a good night's sleep. Unlike bedtime mode, wind down gradually reduces the amount of blue light and notifications on your phone before bedtime. To enable wind down, open the Settings app and select "Digital wellbeing & parental controls." Then, select "Wind down" and toggle it on. You can then customize the hours during which wind down is enabled.

## Focus Mode

Focus mode is another digital wellbeing feature that can help you stay focused and productive. When focus mode is enabled, notifications from selected apps are turned off. To enable focus mode, open the Settings app and select "Digital wellbeing & parental controls." Then, select "Focus mode" and toggle it on. You can select the apps you want to receive notifications while focus mode is enabled.

## Do Not Disturb

Do not disturb mode is a feature that silences notifications and alerts from your phone. To enable do not disturb mode, open the Settings app and select "Do not disturb." Then, tap "Turn on now" to enable the feature immediately or "Schedules" to set a schedule for when do not-disturb mode should be enabled. You can also customize which alerts are allowed when the do-not-disturb mode is enabled.

# CHAPTER 9

# Accessories

There are several great accessories to use with the Google Pixel device. A few are as follows;

## Screen Protectors

Screen protectors are popular accessories for the Pixel. They can help to protect your screen from scratches and cracks. There are a variety of different materials and styles available for screen protectors. There are tempered glass protectors, which are more durable, and plastic protectors, which are usually cheaper and easier to apply. There are even privacy screen protectors, which can help to keep your screen from being seen by others.

## AirPods

AirPods are a popular choice for wireless earbuds and are compatible with the Pixel. They offer excellent sound quality and a long battery life. The AirPods Pro also offers active noise cancellation and transparency mode, which can be helpful in different situations. There are also a variety of other wireless earbuds available for you to use with your Google Pixel.

## Cases

There are a variety of cases available for the Pixel that offers it maximum protection, including clear cases, silicone cases, leather cases, rugged cases, and more. There are even cases designed specifically for certain activities, like hiking or biking. You can also find cases with extra features like card slots or kickstands.

## Pixel Buds

The Pixel Buds are Google's wireless earbuds, and they're explicitly designed to work with the Pixel. They offer excellent sound quality and a comfortable fit. The Pixel Buds also have unique features, like hands-free Google Assistant access and the ability to translate conversations in real time. And if you have a Pixel phone, you can also use the Buds to find your phone if you lose it.

## Lenses

The Pixel has several different lenses that you can use to take photos and videos. There's the standard lens, the wide-angle lens, and the telephoto lens. The standard lens is suitable for everyday photos, the wide-angle lens is good for group shots or landscapes, and the telephoto lens is suitable for zooming in on distant subjects.

## Chargers

There are a few different types of chargers you can use with your Pixel. The most common type is a USB-C charger, which you can use with a USB-C cable. Some chargers also support fast charging, which can quickly charge your phone. There are also tons of wireless charger options available for powering your pixel device.

## CHAPTER 10

# Camera and Videography

The Google Pixel is known for its excellent camera and videography capabilities. The camera has features like Portrait Mode, Night Sight, and Motion Mode, which allow you to take great photos and videos in any lighting situation. You can also use Google's "Top Shot" feature to capture the perfect moment. And with the Pixel's Cinematic Pan feature, you can create smooth panning shots with just a few taps. Some of the features explained;

> **Portrait mode** is a feature that allows you to take professional-looking portraits with a blurred background effect. This feature uses the Pixel's dual-pixel technology and machine learning algorithms to create a realistic blur effect. Portrait mode works best with close-up shots of people, but it can also be used with pets and other subjects.

> **Night Sight** is one of the Pixel's most popular features. It's a low-light mode that allows you to take amazing photos in the dark. Night Sight uses computational photography to create bright, clear images even in the darkest conditions. This feature can also be used for astrophotography, allowing you to take stunning night sky photos.

> **Motion mode** is a feature that lets you capture smooth, cinematic videos with your Pixel. This feature works by combining multiple frames to create a smooth video. Motion mode captures

sports, action scenes, or other fast-moving subjects. The Pixel can also create fun effects with Motion mode, like the "Long Exposure" and "Cinematic Pan" modes.

▶ **Magic Eraser** is a feature that allows you to remove unwanted objects from your photos. This feature uses machine learning to identify and replace unwanted objects with surrounding details. Magic Eraser can remove people, objects, and even more significant elements like cars and buildings. You can also use Magic Eraser to touch up your photos and remove distractions.

## Sharing Pictures and Videos

First, you can use the "Share" button in the Photos app to share directly from your phone. You can also use the "Backup and Sync" feature to automatically backup your photos and videos to Google Photos. You can easily share your photos and videos with friends and family from there.

## Camera Setting

The Pixel has several camera settings to adjust to get the perfect shot. In the camera app, you can change the "Scene Detection" setting to automatically optimize the photo for the type of scene you're shooting. You can also adjust the "HDR+" setting to control the amount of detail and dynamic range in your photos. And if you want to control the brightness, you can use the "Exposure compensation" slider.

## Taking Screenshot

You can use the "Power" and "Volume Down" buttons to take a screenshot on the Pixel. Hold down both buttons for a few seconds, and you'll hear a camera shutter sound. The screenshot will then be saved in the "Screenshots" folder in your "Gallery" app. You can also take a screenshot by swiping down from the top of the screen and tapping the "Screenshot" icon.

## Screen Recording

The Pixel also has a built-in screen recording feature that you can use to capture video of your screen. To start a screen recording, swipe down from the top of the screen and tap the "Screen record" icon. You can choose to include audio and show your touches on the screen. When you're ready to start recording, tap the "Start" button.

# CHAPTER 11

# Troubleshooting Tips

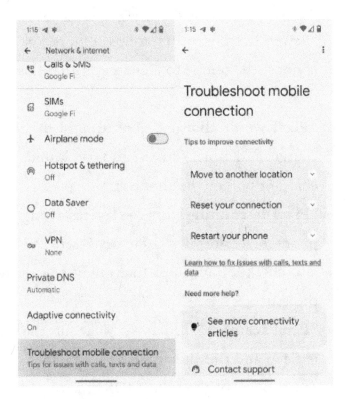

If you're having trouble with your Pixel, you can try a few things to troubleshoot the issue. First, make sure you have the latest software update installed. You can check for updates in the "Settings" app. If you're still having trouble, try restarting your phone or performing a factory reset. You can also contact Google Support for additional help. Below are some common issues that Pixel users experience, along with some troubleshooting tips:

- **"Pixel won't turn on."**—Try holding down the "Power" button for 30 seconds or more. You can connect the phone to a charger if that doesn't work.

- **"Pixel won't charge."**—Try using a different charger and cable. You can also try cleaning the charging port on the phone.

- **"Pixel is running slow."**—Try restarting the phone or performing a factory reset. You can also check for any apps that might be causing the issue.

- **"Pixel's camera is blurry."**—Make sure the lens is clean and free of smudges or scratches. You can also try toggling the "HDR+" setting in the camera app.

▶ **"Pixel's battery drains quickly."**—Make sure the phone isn't overheating, and check for any apps that might be draining the battery. You can also try turning off features like "Always-on display" or "Location services."

www.ingramcontent.com/pod-product-compliance
Lightning Source LLC
LaVergne TN
LVHW051714050326
832903LV00032B/4198

* 9 7 9 8 8 7 4 1 0 5 8 5 3 *